# RICHARD STRAUSS

## METAMORPHOSEN
*a study for 23 solo strings*

## OBOE CONCERTO

## FOUR LAST SONGS

London · New York · Berlin

Cover design by Lynette Williamson
Front cover picture: *Richard Strauss at the conductor's podium, 1929* by Wilhelm Victor Krausz (b. 1878)
    Private Collection/Bridgeman Art Library
Preface © Copyright 2001 by Malcolm MacDonald
Printed and bound in England by Halstan & Co. Ltd, Amersham, Bucks.

# Contents

*Richard Strauss, late 1940s*
Photo: Boosey & Hawkes

# Preface

Richard Strauss completed his last opera, *Capriccio*, in August 1941. He was 77. Yet musical ideas continued to arise, and he still put in a daily stint of compositional work - almost, it seemed, for his own amusement. Thus in the most uncertain years of World War II he began a series of works not so much nostalgic for, as immersed in a dream of, a vanished and more civilized world. This 'Indian Summer', his last period of instrumental compositions and songs, formed a vastly experienced epilogue – by turns sombre, witty and tender – to his output of the previous 60 years.

In August 1944 Strauss began a study for 23 solo strings which he called *Metamorphosen*. The title alludes to Goethe's theories of plant growth, the external shape continually changing while essential identity is unchanged. Strauss's work is really a series of free variations on the funereal idea heard in its opening bars. It is unmistakably a lament – his most intense music of mourning – composed as the war ground slowly to its end. The work is conceived in three large sections, prefaced by a short introduction and concluded by a substantial, elaborately-woven coda. Its argument, however, is grimly continuous, the material growing and evolving across the formal divisions in a continual process of thematic transformation. Each player is treated as a soloist; Strauss creates textures of extra-ordinary refinement, subtle effects of chiaroscuro balancing the broad sweep of the melodic lines. The closing pages quote, in the low strings, the funeral-march theme from Beethoven's *Eroica*; Strauss marked it 'IN MEMORIAM!', as if in farewell to German culture. The idea has been present *in potentia* since the beginning: the theme introduced at bar 9 in the violas is a kind of memory of it, though Strauss claimed he only became aware of the resemblance during the process of composition.

Just after the close of the war John de Lancie, an American GI stationed in Bavaria, Germany (and in civilian life the first oboist of the Pittsburgh Orchestra), was bold enough to approach Strauss to request 'an oboe piece'. Strauss responded with a full-scale concerto, the last music he drafted in Germany before he moved to Switzerland (where it was completed at the end of October 1945). The première took place in Zürich on 26 February 1946 (Marcel Saillet was the soloist) – a month after Paul Sacher conducted the first performance of *Metamorphosen* with the Zürich Collegium Musicum. Strauss significantly revised the ending of the work for publication in 1948.

Of all the 'Indian Summer' compositions this is the most serene, but it is also a true virtuoso concerto requiring considerable control and bravura from the soloist. The first movement begins almost in the manner of a Mozart comic-opera overture, the scurrying orchestra forming a background to the oboe's free-spinning, capriciously lyrical cantilena. It is very rich in invention, and – in a manner which recalls the techniques, if not the mood, of *Metamorphosen* – several of its themes are further developed in the lush central Andante movement, which grows out of the first without a break and culminates in the work's principal cadenza. The finale starts as a scherzo-like rondo movement in 2/4 which leads to a second cadenza; this in turn introduces not a coda, but a liltingly elegant Allegro in 6/8 which eventually leads back to the scherzo-like music and the Concerto's witty concluding bars.

The collection of songs for voice and orchestra published as *Four Last Songs* was first performed in London on 22 May 1950 by Kirsten Flagstad and the Philharmonia Orchestra, conducted by Furtwängler. Strauss had died the previous year, aged 85, and had not indicated the order of the songs or a general title: these matters were resolved by his publisher Ernst Roth. 'Im Abendrot', to a text by Eichendorff, was sketched in 1946-7; Strauss then put it aside for a year, completing the full score only in May 1948; the other songs, to poems by Hermann Hesse, were then quite rapidly composed in the order 'Frühling', 'Beim Schlafengehen' and 'September'. The collection has rightly been viewed as the summit of his long lifetime of lieder-writing. The highly elaborate orchestration provides a sumptuously autumnal glow (even in 'Frühling', whose carolling birds celebrate Spring) to irradiate the soaring and ecstatic vocal line with its melodic melismas and simple, ruminatively curving phrases. Despite its very wide compass, the solo part is completely integrated with the other instruments in an almost ideal fusion of vocal and orchestral colour. As 'Im Abendrot' draws to a close, at the question 'can this perhaps be death?' the orchestra quotes the 'Transfiguration' theme from his early tone-poem *Death and Transfiguration*, suggesting that the answer is in the affirmative, but that something may lie beyond.

Malcolm MacDonald

# Préface

Richard Strauss acheva son dernier opéra, *Capriccio*, en août 1941, à l'âge de soixante-dix-sept ans. Il ne manquait pourtant pas d'inspiration et continua de travailler tous les jours, presque, semblait-il, par plaisir personnel. Ainsi, durant les années les plus incertaines de la deuxième guerre mondiale, il commença une série d'œuvres non pas vraiment nostalgiques, mais plutôt plongées dans le songe d'un monde disparu et plus civilisé. Cet « été indien », sa dernière période de composition d'œuvres instrumentales et de lieder, constitua l'épilogue, véritable trésor d'expérience tour à tour sombre, léger et tendre, de soixante années de création musicale.

En août 1944, Strauss commença une étude pour vingt-trois instruments à cordes solistes qu'il intitula *Metamorphosen*. Ce titre fait référence aux théories de Goethe sur la croissance des végétaux, leur forme externe subissant une perpétuelle mutation alors que leur identité essentielle ne change pas. Cette œuvre de Strauss est de fait une série de variations libres sur le thème funèbre des premières mesures. Il s'agit là indéniablement d'une élégie, de sa plus intense musique de deuil, composée alors que la guerre touchait lentement à sa fin. Cette œuvre comprend trois parties préfacées d'une courte introduction et se termine par une coda substantielle et élaborée. Néanmoins, son argument est sombrement continu, le matériau se développe et évolue par delà les divisions formelles, suivant un processus constant de transformation thématique. Chaque musicien y est un soliste. Strauss crée des textures d'un extraordinaire raffinement, des effets subtils de clair-obscur qui répondent à l'amplitude des lignes mélodiques. Les dernières pages reprennent, aux cordes graves, le thème de la marche funèbre de la Symphonie Héroïque de Beethoven. Sur la partition, Strauss a indiqué « IN MEMORIAM! » , comme s'il faisait ses adieux à la culture allemande. Cette notion est présente sous forme latente dès le début : le thème qui commence à la mesure 9 aux altos en est une sorte de souvenir, bien que Strauss ait déclaré ne s'être aperçu de cette ressemblance qu'au cours de la composition.

Juste après la fin de la guerre, John de Lancie, un GI américain stationné en Bavière (et dans le civil, premier hautbois de l'Orchestre symphonique de Pittsburgh), eut suffisamment d'audace pour lui réclamer un « morceau pour hautbois » . Strauss répondit à cette demande en écrivant un concerto entier, sa dernière œuvre ébauchée en Allemagne avant son départ pour la Suisse (où il la termina à la fin du mois d'octobre 1945). La création de ce concerto eut lieu le 26 février 1946 (Marcel Saillet était le soliste), un mois après celle de *Metamorphosen* dirigée par Paul Sacher avec le Zürich Collegium Musicum. Strauss fit des changements significatifs à la fin de l'œuvre pour sa publication en 1948.

De toutes les compositions de « l'été indien », cette œuvre est la plus sereine, mais c'est également un concerto véritablement virtuose qui requiert un contrôle et une bravoure considérables de la part du soliste. Le premier mouvement débute presque à la manière d'une ouverture d'opéra comique de Mozart, l'orchestre rapide et agile formant un arrière-plan musical à la cantilène librement et capricieusement lyrique du hautbois. Strauss déploie des trésors d'invention et, dans un style rappelant les techniques, sinon l'atmosphère, des *Metamorphosen*, développe plusieurs de ses thèmes dans le splendide mouvement central Andante, lequel naît sans interruption du premier et conduit à la cadence principale de l'œuvre. Le final commence comme un rondo de style scherzo en 2/4 et mène à une seconde cadence qui, à son tour, introduit non pas une coda, mais un allegro au rythme élégant en 6/8, lequel nous ramène finalement à la musique de style scherzo et aux mesures légères de la fin du concerto.

La création du recueil de lieder pour voix et orchestre publié sous le titre *Quatre Dernièrs Mélodies* eut lieu le 22 mai 1950 à Londres sous la direction de Furtwängler, avec Kirsten Flagstad et le Philharmonia Orchestra. Strauss s'était éteint l'année précédente, à l'âge de quatre-vingt-cinq ans, sans avoir indiqué l'ordre des lieder, ni donné de titre général. Ces questions furent réglées par son éditeur, Ernst Roth. « Im Abendrot », sur un texte d'Eichendorff, fut ébauché en 1946-1947, puis Strauss l'abandonna pendant un an pour ne l'achever qu'en mai 1948. Après cela les autres lieder, sur des textes d'Hermann Hesse, furent composées rapidement dans l'ordre suivant : « Frühling », « Beim Schlafengehen » et « September ». Ce recueil est considéré, à juste titre, comme l'apogée de sa longue carrière de compositeur de lieder. L'orchestration extrêmement élaborée présente un éclat somptueusement automnal (même dans « Frühling », dont les chants d'oiseaux célèbrent le printemps) qui irradie la ligne vocale extatique, ses mélismes et ses phrases simples, courbes, contemplatives. Malgré la tessiture étendue qu'elle requiert, la partie soliste est entièrement intégrée aux autres instruments dans une fusion presque idéale de couleur vocale et orchestrale. Vers la fin de « Im Abendrot », à la question « Ceci, est-ce donc la mort ? » , l'orchestre reprend le thème de la « Transfiguration » du poème symphonique des débuts de Strauss *Mort et Transfiguration*, ce qui suggère que la réponse est affirmative, mais que quelque chose se trouve peut-être au-delà.

Malcolm MacDonald

# Vorwort

Richard Strauss vollendete seine letzte Oper *Capriccio* im August 1941. Er war 77 Jahre alt. Dennoch, der Strom musikalischer Ideen floss weiter und Strauss blieb seinem täglichen Arbeitspensum treu – doch eher zu seinem eigenen Vergnügen, wie es schien. So begann er in den besonders ungewissen Jahren des 2. Weltkriegs eine Reihe von Werken, weniger in Sehnsucht nach als vielmehr umfangen vom Traum von einer versunkenen, zivilisierteren Welt. Dieser 'Indian Summer', eine letzte Schaffensperiode von Instrumentalkompositionen und Liedern, brachte einen in jeder Hinsicht ausgereiften Epilog zu seinem Schaffen der vorherigen 60 Jahre hervor - abwechselnd düster, amüsant und empfindsam.

Im August 1944 begann Strauss eine Studie für 23 Solostreicher und gab ihr den Titel *Metamorphosen*. Dieser Titel spielt auf Goethes Theorie über das Pflanzenwachstum an, bei der sich die äußere Gestalt zwar fortwährend ändert, die zur Wesenheit gehörige Identität jedoch nicht. In der Tat stellt Strauss' Werk eine Reihe freier Variationen über eine trauermarschartige Idee aus den ersten Takten des Werkes dar. Das Stück ist unverkennbar ein Lamento – Strauss' eindringlichste Trauermusik – , geschrieben, während sich der Krieg seinem Ende zu schleppte. Das Werk ist in drei umfangreichen Teilen angelegt; vorangestellt ist eine kurze Einleitung, den Schluss bildet eine kunstvoll gesponnene Coda. Der eigentliche Gegenstand des Werkes aber ist unbarmherzig präsent, das Material wächst und entwickelt sich über die formalen Abschnitte hinweg in einem kontinuierlichen Prozess der thematischen Transformation. Jeder Spieler ist wie ein Solist behandelt; Strauss erzeugt Texturen von außerordentlicher Feinheit, subtile Helldunkel-Effekte gestalten harmonisch die weitläufigen Wendungen der melodischen Linien. Die letzten Seiten zitieren in den tiefen Streichern das Thema des Trauermarsches aus Beethovens *Eroica*; Strauss versah diese Takte mit der Bemerkung 'IN MEMORIAM!', wie ein Lebewohl an die deutsche Kultur. Dieser Gedanke als solcher war *in potentia* schon von Beginn des Stückes an gegenwärtig: das Thema in Takt 9 in den Violen erinnert daran. Strauss behauptete gleichwohl, er hätte die Ähnlichkeit erst während des Prozesses der Komposition bemerkt.

Gleich nach dem Ende des Krieges fragte John de Lancie, ein in Bayern stationierter amerikanischer Soldat (und als Zivilist 1. Oboist des Pittsburgh Symphony Orchestra), bei Richard Strauss frank heraus nach einem "Oboenstück". Strauss antwortete mit einem ausgewachsenen Oboenkonzert, dem letzten Stück, das er in Deutschland vor seinem Weggang in die Schweiz begann (er vollendete es dort Ende Oktober 1945). Die Uraufführung fand am 26. Februar 1946 in Zürich statt (Marcel Saillet war der Solist) – einen Monat, nachdem Paul Sacher die Uraufführung der *Metamorphosen* mit dem Zürcher Collegium Musicum dirigiert hatte. Für die Veröffentlichung im Jahr 1948 führte Strauss umfangreiche Revisionen am Schluss des Stückes durch.

Von allen 'Indian Summer'-Kompositionen ist diese die heiterste, dennoch handelt es sich um ein veritables Virtuosenstück, das vom Solisten einiges an Beherrschung und Bravour verlangt. Der 1. Satz beginnt fast wie die Ouvertüre einer komischen Mozart-Oper, das dahin huschende Orchester bildet den Hintergrund für die weit gesponnene, kapriziös lyrische Kantilene. Ein Satz reich an Erfindung – in einer Weise, die an die Techniken, sogar an die Stimmung der *Metamorphosen* erinnert –, und einige seiner Themen werden im üppigen Andante-Mittelsatz weiter entwickelt, der ohne Pause aus dem 1. Satz erwächst und seinen Höhepunkt bei der Hauptkadenz des Werkes erreicht. Das Finale beginnt wie ein scherzohafter Rondo-satz im 2/4-Takt und mündet in eine zweite Kadenz; diese wiederum leitet nicht eine Coda, sondern in ein leichtfüßig-elegantes Allegro im 6/8-Takt, das schließlich zurück zum Scherzocharakter und den geistreichen Schlusstakten führt.

Die Serie von Orchesterliedern, veröffentlicht unter dem Titel *Vier letzte Lieder*, wurde am 22. Mai 1950 in London durch Kirsten Flagstad und das Philharmonia Orchestra unter der Leitung von Wilhelm Furtwängler uraufgeführt. Strauss war im Jahr zuvor mit 85 Jahren gestorben und hatte weder Anzeichen für eine Anordnung der Lieder noch für einen Titel hinterlassen; sein Verleger Ernst Roth nahm die Regelung dieser Fragen in die Hand. 'Im Abendrot' auf einen Text von Eichendorff wurde in den Jahren 1946/47 entworfen; Strauss legte es dann für ein Jahr zur Seite und stellte die Partitur erst im Mai 1948 fertig; die anderen Lieder nach Gedichten von Hermann Hesse entstanden dann in ziemlich schneller Folge: 'Frühling', 'Beim Schlafengehen' und 'September'. Diese Lieder sind zurecht als der Gipfel Strausscher Liedkunst angesehen worden. Die mit größter Sorgfalt ausgearbeitete Instrumentation lässt einen prachtvoll herbstlichen Glanz (sogar in 'Frühling' mit seinen zwitschernden Vögeln) die sich hoch aufschwingende, schwärmerische Gesangslinie mit ihren melodischen Melismen und einfach gehaltenen, nachdenklich schweifenden Phrasen bescheinen. Trotz des sehr großen Stimmumfangs ist der Gesangspart vollkommen in das instrumentale Geschehen eingebettet in einer nahezu idealen Verschmelzung vokaler und orchestraler Farben. Wenn 'Im Abendrot' zum Abschluss findet, mit der Frage 'ist dies etwa der Tod?', zitiert das Orchester das 'Verklärungs'-Thema aus Strauss' früher Tondichtung *Tod und Verklärung*, nahelegend, dass die Antwort nur "ja" sein kann, dass etwas jedoch noch dahinter sein könnte.

Malcolm MacDonald

# METAMORPHOSEN

*Instrumentation*

10 Violins
5 Violas
5 Violoncellos
3 Double Basses

Duration: c. 30 minutes

*Paul Sacher und dem Collegium Musicum Zürich gewidmet*

1

# METAMORPHOSEN

RICHARD STRAUSS

*Begonnen 13. März 1945*

poco più mosso

160
Vl. 1
Vl. 2
Vl. 3
Vla. 1
Vla. 2
Vla. 3
Vla. 4
Vc. 1
Vc. 2
Vc. 3
Vc. 4
Cb. 1
p
cresc.
f

180

Agitato

noch etwas lebhafter

46

B. & H. 9118

52

B. & H. 9118

56

B.& H. 9118

Più allegro

accelerando

390

Adagio, tempo primo

**430** tempo primo

ritard. 500

GARMISCH, 12. April 1945

B. & H. 9118

# RICHARD STRAUSS
# OBOE CONCERTO

*Instrumentation*

2 Flutes
English Horn
2 Clarinets in B♭
2 Bassoons
2 Horns in F
Strings

Duration: c. 23 minutes

*Meinem Freunde Dr. Volkmar Andreae*
*und dem Tonhalleorchester in Zürich gewidmet*

# CONCERTO FOR OBOE
## and small orchestra

Konzert für Oboe und kleines orchester. | Concerto pour hautbois et petit orchestre

RICHARD STRAUSS

B. & H. 16388

98

B.& H. 16388

Fl. I. II
I
Cl. in Sib
II
I
Fag.
II
Cor. II in Fa
Ob. Solo
Vl. I
Vl. II
Vle.
Vc.
Cb.
cresc.
arco
pizz.
10
Fl. I. II
Cl. I in Sib
Fag. I. II
Cor. II in Fa
Ob. Solo
Vl. I
Vl. II
Vle.
Vc.
Cb.

Fag. I
Ob. Solo
Vl. I
Vl. II
Vle.
Vc.
Cb.
27
Cl. I. II in Sib
Fag. I. II
p
Ob. Solo
Vl. I
Vl. II
Vle.
Vc.
Cb.
28
C. I.
p espr.
Cl. I. II in Sib
Fag. I. II
28
Ob. Solo
p espr.
Vl. II
Vle.
p

Fl. I. II
Cl. I. II in Si♭
Fag. I. II
Cor. I. II in Fa
Ob. Solo
Vl. I
Vl. II
Vle.
Vc.
Cb.
a2
pizz.
Cadenza

B. & H. 16888

130

Cl.I
in Sib
Fag.I.II
Ob.Solo
Vl.I
Vl.II
Vle.
I
Vc.
II
Vc.
III.IV
Cb.
cresc.
p
39
C.I.
Cl.I.II
in Sib
Fag.I.II
Cor.I
in Fa
espr.
pp
Ob.Solo
Vl.I
Vl.II
Vle.
I
Vc.
II
Vc.
III.IV
Cb.
Solo
p espr.

Fl. I
C.I.
Cl. I. II in Sib
Fag. I. II
Cor. II in Fa
Ob. Solo
Vl. I
Vl. II
Vle.
Solo
Vc.
G.A.
Cb.
42
Fl. I
Cl. I. II in Sib
Fag. I. II
a2
Ob. Solo
Vl. I
Vl. II
Vle.
Solo
Tutti
Vc.
Cb.

B.&H. 16388

B. & H. 16388

150

151

B. & H. 16388

B. & H. 16388

B.& H. 16388

# FOUR LAST SONGS
## *Song listing and instrumentation*

2 Flutes, 2 Oboes, English Horn, 2 Clarinets in A,
Bass Clarinet in A, 3 Bassoons, 4 Horns, Harp, Strings

3 Flutes, 2 Oboes, English Horn, 2 Clarinets in B♭,
Bass Clarinet in B♭, 2 Bassoons, 2 Horns in F, 2 Horns in D,
2 Trumpets in C, Harp, Strings

2 Piccolos, 2 Flutes, 2 Oboes, English Horn, 2 Clarinets in B♭,
Bass Clarinet in B♭, 2 Bassoons, 4 Horns in F, 2 Trumpets in F,
3 Trombones, Tuba, Celesta, Strings

2 Flutes (both doubling Piccolos), 2 Oboes, English Horn,
2 Clarinets in B♭, Bass Clarinet in B♭, 2 Bassoons,
Double Bassoon, 2 Horns in F, 2 Horns in E♭, 3 Trumpets in E♭,
3 Trombones, Tuba, Timpani, Strings

Total duration: c. 22 minutes

# FOUR LAST SONGS
## translation of German texts

## Spring (Hermann Hesse)

In half-light I waited,
Dreamed all too long
Of trees in blossom,
Those flowing breezes,
That fragrant blue
And thrushes' song.

Now streaming and glowing
From sky to field
With light overflowing
All these charms are revealed.

Light gilds the river,
Light floods the plain;
Spring calls me: and through me there
    quiver
Life's own loveliness,
Life's own sweetness returned again!

## September (Hermann Hesse)

These mournful flowers,
Rain-drenched in the coolness are bending,
While Summer cowers,
Mute as he waits for his ending.

Gravely each golden leaf
Falls from the tallest Acacia tree;
Summer marvels and smiles to see
His own garden grow faint with grief.

Ling'ring still, near the roses long he stays,
Longs for repose;
Languid, slow to the last,
His weary eyelids close.

## Time to Sleep (Hermann Hesse)

Now the day has wearied me,
All my gain and all my longing
Like a weary child's shall be
Night whose many stars are thronging.

Hands, now leave your work alone;
Brow, forget your idle thinking,
All my thoughts, their labour done,
Softly into sleep are sinking.

High the soul will rise in flight,
Freely gliding, softly swaying,
In the magic realm of night,
Deeper laws of life obeying.

## At Dusk (Joseph von Eichendorff)

Here both in need and gladness
We wandered hand in hand;
Now let us pause at last
Above the silent land.

Dusk comes the vales exploring,
The darkling air grows still,
Alone two skylarks soaring
In song their dreams fulfil.

Draw close and leave them singing,
Soon will be time to sleep,
How lost our way's beginning!
This solitude, how deep.

O rest so long desired!
We sense the night's soft breath
Now we are tired, how tired!
Can this perhaps be death?

Translation by Michael Hamburger

# QUATRE DERNIÈRES MÉLODIES
## traduction des textes allemands

## Le printemps (Hermann Hesse)

Dans la pénombre des vallées,
J'ai longuement rêvé de tes arbres et de ton air
   bleu,
De tes parfums et de ton ramage.

Maintenant tu es épanoui dans toute ta gloire,
Inondé de lumière,
Comme un miracle devant mes yeux.

Tu me reconnais,
Tu me séduis doucement;
Mes membres frémissent
Face à ta suave présence.

## Septembre (Hermann Hesse)

Le jardin est en deuil,
La fraîche pluie pénètre les fleurs.
L'été frissonne en touchant
Silencieusement à sa fin.

Les feuilles dorées tombent
L'une après l'autre du haut acacia.
L'été sourit, surpris et las
Dans le rêve du jardin expirant.

Longtemps, il reste près des roses,
Désirant ardemment le repos.
Lentement, il ferme ses yeux fatigués.

## Au coucher (Hermann Hesse)

Maintenant que la journée a épuisé mes forces,
Fasse que la nuit constellée d'étoiles accueille
Mon désir de repos
Comme celui d'un enfant fatigué.

Mains, cessez toute activité,
Front, délaisse toute pensée.
Tous mes sens désirent
Plonger dans le sommeil.

Et l'âme sans garde
Veut planer en vol libre,
Pour vivre mille fois plus intensément
Dans le cercle magique de la nuit.

## Au crépuscule
## (Joseph von Eichendorff)

Nous avons traversé la misère et le bonheur
   ensemble,
La main dans la main;
Maintenant nous nous reponsons après le voyage,
Au-dessus du pays silencieux.

Autour de nous, les vallées s'inclinent,
Et l'air s'assombrit déjà.
Seules, deux alouettes, comme dans un rêve,
Montent dans l'air parfumé.

Viens, laisse-les tournoyer.
Bientôt, il sera temps de dormir,
Et il ne faut pas nous égarer
Dans cette solitude.

O grande, calme paix, si profonde
Dans la rougeur du crépuscule.
Comme nous sommes las de voyager.
Ceci, est-ce donc la mort?

Traduction Jesper Overgaard
© SteepleChase Productions ApS

*Dr. Willi Schuh und Frau gewidmet*

# FRÜHLING

(Hermann Hesse)

RICHARD STRAUSS

Performing rights reserved by the composer
Droits d'exécution réservés par le compositeur
Aufführungsrecht vom Komponisten vorbehalten

dämm - ri - gen Grüf - ten träum - te ich lang.............................. von dei - nen

162

164

B. & H. 16921

166

B. & H. 16921

- wart! .........................

B. & H. 16921

# SEPTEMBER

(Hermann Hesse)

RICHARD STRAUSS

Performing rights reserved by the composer
Droits d'exécution réservés par le compositeur
Aufführungsrecht vom Komponisten vorbehalten

trau - ert, Kühl........ sinkt in die Blu - - - - - men der Re - gen.

ben-den Gar - - - ten-traum.

*Herrn und Frau Dr. Adolf Jöhr gewidmet*

# BEIM SCHLAFENGEHN

(Hermann Hesse)

RICHARD STRAUSS

Nun der Tag - mich müd ge-macht,

Performing rights reserved by the composer
Droits d'exécution réservés par le compositeur
Aufführungsrecht vom Komponisten vorbehalten

soll mein sehn - li-ches Ver - lan-gen freund lich die ge-stirn-te Nacht wie ein mü - des Kind ..................... em-

al - les Den - ken, al - le mei - ne Sin - ne nun wol-len sich in Schlum -

190

B. & H. 16920

F
pp subito
Picc. I. II
Fl. I. II
Oboi I. II
C. I.
Cl. I. II in Sib
Cl. b. in Sib
I Fag. II
I. II Cor. in Fa
III Cor. in Fa IV
Trbe. I. II in Fa
I Tromb. II & III
Tuba
Celesta
Voce
- - en Flü - - - gen schwe - - ben, um im
Vl. I
Vl. II
I Vle. II
I Vcl. II
C. B.
cresc.

Pontresina, 4. August 1948

*Dr. Ernst Roth gewidmet*

# IM ABENDROT

(Joseph von Eichendorff)

RICHARD STRAUSS

- dern ru - - hen wir............ nun ü-berm stil - len Land. Rings sich die